ABANDONED PLACES

SKARA BRAE

THE LOST NEOLITHIC VILLAGE

BY LISA OWINGS

TORQUE
™

Torque brims with excitement perfect for thrill-seekers of all kinds. Discover daring survival skills, explore uncharted worlds, and marvel at mighty engines and extreme sports. In *Torque* books, anything can happen. Are you ready?

This edition first published in 2020 by Bellwether Media, Inc.

No part of this publication may be reproduced in whole or in part without written permission of the publisher. For information regarding permission, write to Bellwether Media, Inc., Attention: Permissions Department, 6012 Blue Circle Drive, Minnetonka, MN 55343.

Library of Congress Cataloging-in-Publication Data

Names: Owings, Lisa, author.
Title: Skara Brae : the Lost Neolithic Village / by Lisa Owings.
Description: Minneapolis : Bellwether Media, 2020. | Series: Torque:
   abandoned places | Includes bibliographical references and index. |
   Audience: Ages 7-12 | Audience: Grades 4-6 | Summary: "Amazing
   photography accompanies engaging information about Skara Brae. The
   combination of high-interest subject matter and light text is intended
   for students in grades 3 through 7"– Provided by publisher.
Identifiers: LCCN 2019030419 (print) | LCCN 2019030420 (ebook) | ISBN
   9781644871645 (library binding) | ISBN 9781618918345 (ebook)
Subjects: LCSH: Skara Brae Site (Scotland)–Juvenile literature. |
   Neolithic period–Scotland–Orkney–Juvenile literature.
Classification: LCC GN776.22.G7 O95 2020 (print) | LCC GN776.22.G7
   (ebook) | DDC 936.1/132–dc23
LC record available at https://lccn.loc.gov/2019030419
LC ebook record available at https://lccn.loc.gov/2019030420

Editor: Betsy Rathburn   Designer: Brittany McIntosh

Printed in the United States of America, North Mankato, MN.

TABLE OF CONTENTS

BACK TO THE STONE AGE

Standing in this ancient village is like being in a time machine. The walls are more than 5,000 years old!

An open area holds a fire pit. Early humans once gathered on stone benches around it. They slept in the beds along the walls. Their blankets were animal skins!

Stone slab shelves were built against the far wall. They once held finely crafted tools, pots, and sacred objects.

Carved in Stone

Scientists found four stone balls at Skara Brae. They were covered in strange carvings. No one knows what they were for. Some think they were signs of religion.

The ruins of Skara Brae paint a vivid picture of how villagers once lived. But what secrets were lost here? What mysteries have these stone walls guarded all this time?

HIDDEN UNDER DUNES

Skara Brae was built on Mainland, the largest
of Scotland's Orkney Islands. It lay hidden
under grass-covered dunes for centuries.

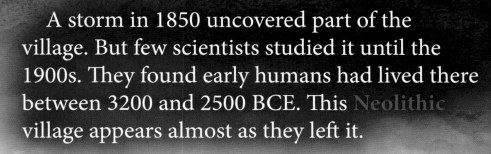

A storm in 1850 uncovered part of the village. But few scientists studied it until the 1900s. They found early humans had lived there between 3200 and 2500 BCE. This Neolithic village appears almost as they left it.

Skara Brae,
Orkney Islands,
Scotland

N
W — E
S

The people of Skara Brae lived in a peaceful community. They farmed, hunted, and fished. Inside their stone walls, they cooked meals and made tools. They even had time to play games and make art.

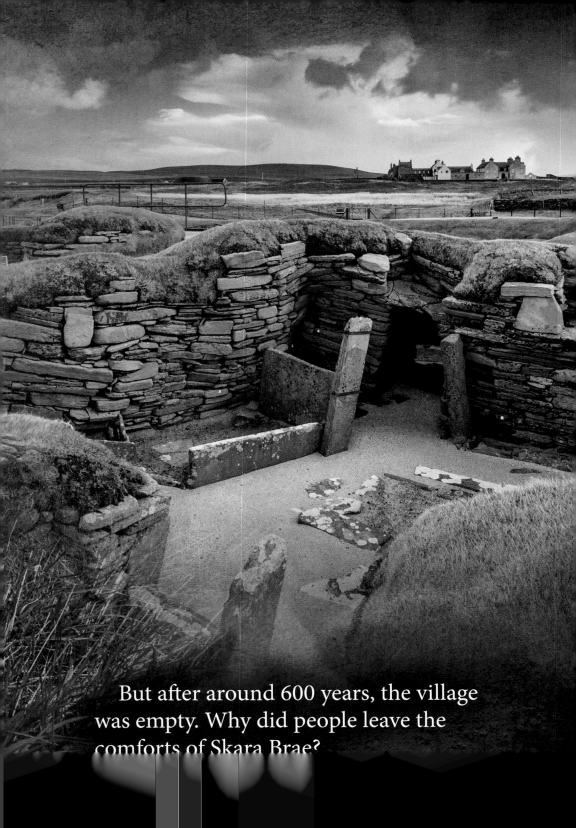

But after around 600 years, the village was empty. Why did people leave the comforts of Skara Brae?

PEACEFUL FARMERS

People arrived in Skara Brae sometime after 3200 BCE. They soon began building the first of eight buildings that would make up their village. The buildings were connected by stone-covered passages.

All the Comforts of Home

Skara Brae has some of the earliest indoor toilets ever found!

Whalebone beams supported earthen roofs. Midden was piled against stone walls for warmth. Skara Brae became a cozy village of 50 to 100 people.

House Eight

Skara Brae's eighth building was likely the village workshop. Instead of beds and shelves, it has empty nooks. Its floors were found covered in stone scraps.

Villagers grew wheat and barley in nearby fields. They raised cows and sheep. Villagers also hunted, fished, and gathered whatever they could find. Stone tanks inside the homes likely

Villagers used all parts of the animals.
Skins provided clothing and blankets.
They made tools out of teeth and bones.

bone tools

15

If Not Stone, Then Bone

The bone dice made at Skara Brae look much like modern dice. Villagers also made jewelry out of animal bones.

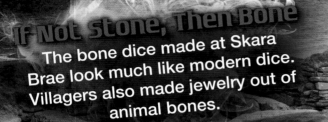

SKARA BRAE TIMELINE

3200–3100 BCE:
Early humans settle in and around Skara Brae

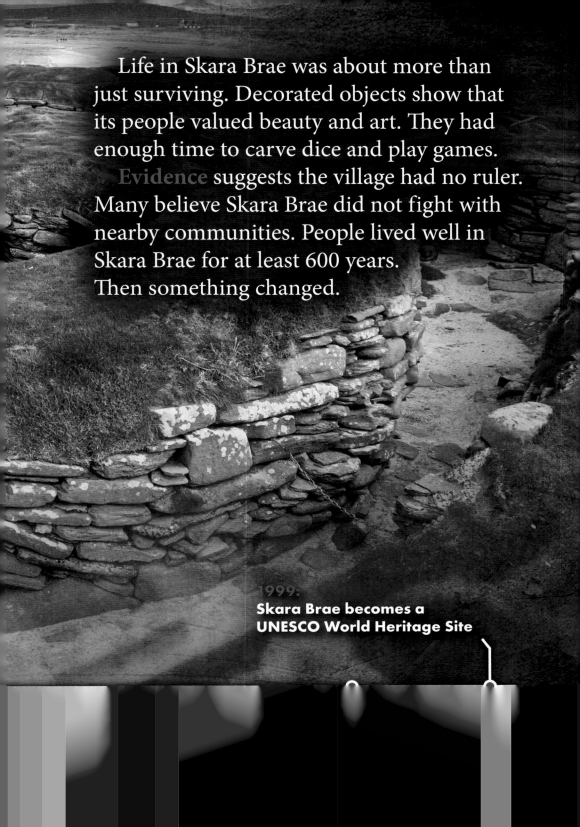

Life in Skara Brae was about more than just surviving. Decorated objects show that its people valued beauty and art. They had enough time to carve dice and play games.

Evidence suggests the village had no ruler. Many believe Skara Brae did not fight with nearby communities. People lived well in Skara Brae for at least 600 years. Then something changed.

1999:
Skara Brae becomes a UNESCO World Heritage Site

BURIED IN THE SAND

No one knows exactly why Skara Brae was abandoned. Early scientists believed it happened suddenly. They thought a storm threatened to bury the village in sand.

Others saw signs of a slower change. Perhaps the slow buildup of garbage, sand, and salt made the land less fertile. Over time, villagers may have left to find richer soil.

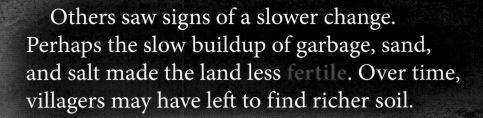

The Broken Necklace

An early scientist found a broken necklace in one of Skara Brae's doorways. He believed the woman wearing it fled a storm. She appeared never to have stopped to pick up the fallen beads.

A Treeless Island

The Orkney Islands are mostly treeless. Villagers likely made most fires with seaweed and animal dung. Any driftwood found along the shore was precious.

Another theory is that Skara Brae came under the control of outside rulers. Perhaps villagers left or were forced to join a larger community

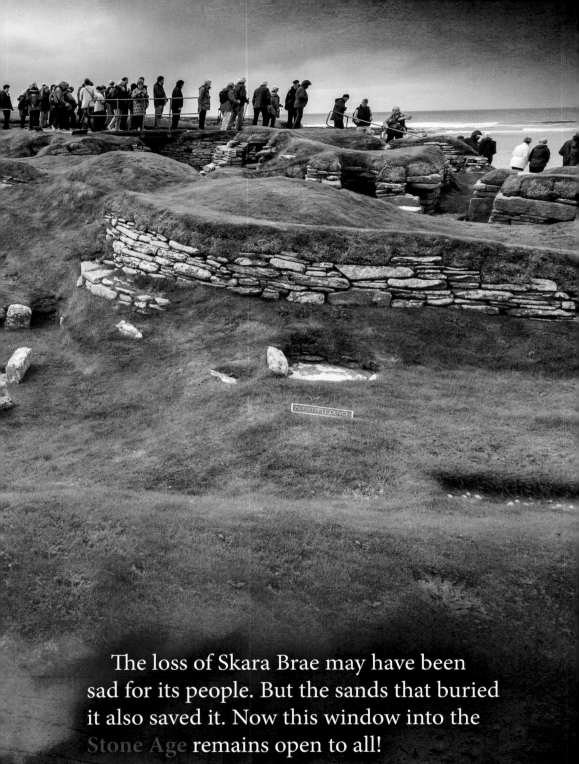

The loss of Skara Brae may have been
sad for its people. But the sands that buried
it also saved it. Now this window into the
Stone Age remains open to all!

GLOSSARY

dunes—sand hills formed by wind or waves

evidence—signs or facts that show something is true

fertile—good for growing food crops or other plants

midden—piles of trash and other waste

Neolithic—the last period of the Stone Age; Neolithic peoples farmed and made tools of polished stone.

ruins—the remains of human-made structures

sacred—very important or holy

Stone Age—the broad prehistoric period when the earliest known humans lived and made stone tools

theory—an idea meant to explain how or why something happens

threatened—showed signs that something harmful or dangerous might happen

vivid—bright and strong

TO LEARN MORE

AT THE LIBRARY

Finch, Dawn. *Skara Brae*. Oxford, U.K.: Raintree, 2016.

Hubbard, Ben. *The Stone Age and Skara Brae*. London, U.K.: Hachette Children's, 2019.

Lock, Deborah. *Life in the Stone Age*. New York, N.Y.: DK Publishing, 2018.

ON THE WEB

FACTSURFER

Factsurfer.com gives you a safe, fun way to find more information.

1. Go to www.factsurfer.com.

2. Enter "Skara Brae" into the search box and click 🔍.

3. Select your book cover to see a list of related web sites.

INDEX